AHHHH
I'M SO BORED!

Activity Book for Teens

This Book Belongs to

_____

>MADE BY TEENS<

CHRISTMAS EDITION

2

WELCOME AND THANK YOU
FOR PURCHASING THIS PAPERBACK BOOK

For more from Gamer Girl Pro and the Made By Teens Series use this QR code here!

Serious Note

Gamer Girl is not responsible for any other form of this books binding outside of the perfect binding type Amazon offers for our books. Spiral bound or any other form outside of the paperback was not created or product tested by Gamer Girl. We take product reprint or rebinding very seriously and will be looking into this matter to make sure our customers get the best for the best price.

We will never ask you to pay more than the listed paperback price no matter the binding type.

We want our books to be affordable for all!

INSTRUCTIONS

Make a mess of this book!

Play with your friends or alone to pass the time.

Each game has individual instructions.

Solutions to puzzles are in the back of the book

Most of all have fun!

EVER OR NEVER

This game is about getting to know your friends and sharing your experiences.

1. There are 20 experience questions. Read each question out loud. Each person has to answer yes or no.

2. For every yes answer you receive an experience point. Whether the experiences are good or bad does not matter.

3. The person with the most experience points wins!

4. To enhance the game, randomly select a person to share the experience they had for each question.

SANTA SOS

Help Santa send an SOS!
The goal is to be the player that connects the most SOS patterns.

Players take turns writing either an **S** or an **O** in a spot on the grid.
If a player makes an SOS sequence, they can use a marker to highlight it in their color and take another turn.
Game ends when the paper is completely full.
The player with the most SOS sequences wins the game..

THE GAME OF SIM

Two players take turns drawing any uncolored lines with each using a different color dot to dot.
Try to avoid the creation of a triangle made solely of your color.
- Intersections of lines are not relevant.
The first player to complete a triangle loses immediately.

FIND THAT WORD

Find that word is a game about finding as many words as you can in a certain time frame. For this book we will say 3 minutes. You can make it longer if needed based on age and skill level.

1. Letters must be touching in a chain that is horizontal, vertical, or diagonal.
2. You can use a letter box only once in a chain.
3. Must have at least 3 letters to score.

Scoring

3 or 4 letters......1 point

5 letters......2 points

6 letters......3 points

7 letters......4 points

8 or more is 10 points

Play alone for fun OR with 2 or more players.

SUDOKU

Sudoku is a single player logic puzzle using numbers. You are given a 9x9 grid with numbers in random places based off of difficulty level. The object is to place the numbers 1 through 9 so that

1. Each row and column have numbers 1 through 9.
2. Each box; 3x3 square have numbers 1 through 9.
3. With no repeats in the same row, column, or box.

EVER OR NEVER

	Yes	No
1. Gone ice skating outside?		
2. Gone sledding with friends?		
3. Helped decorate a Christmas tree?		
4. Had a secret Santa gift exchange?		
5. Built a snowman?		
6. Had hot coffee on a cold day?		
7. Had a snowball fight?		
8. Hosted a Christmas movie marathon?		
9. Tried skiing?		
10. Baked Christmas cookies?		
11. Went to a Christmas party?		
12. Tried snowboarding?		
13. Gone caroling with a group?		
14. Wrapped presents for someone else?		
15. Done a winter photoshoot outside?		
16. Helped a charity during the holidays?		
17. Had a real Christmas Tree?		
18. Worn an ugly sweater?		
19. Slept all day on winter break?		
20. Gone shopping for gifts?		

Points total:

WORD SEARCH 1
Christmas Morning

```
C A M M W W F A M I L Y
O T U N P R E S E N T S
O K S X A A S U E H R E
K A I Z J P T R E E A H
I B C I A P I P Y X D L
E F A M M I V R B J I A
S V N J A N E I J A T U
F S D D S G F S X C I G
I L L D V X T E G B O H
P Q E X C I T E M E N T
N H S T O C K I N G S E
X U W A R M T H U B I R
```

Candles   Laughter   Surprise
Cookies   Music   Traditions
Excitement   Pajamas   Tree
Family   Presents   Warmth
Festive   Stockings   Wrapping

THE GAME OF SiM

MAZE #1

Start

Finish

XMAS WORDPLAY

Christmas Shopping Adventure

It was a _____ winter day when my friends and I decided to go
ADJECTIVE

Christmas shopping at the_____. We bundled up in our_____ coats
PLACE   COLOR

and hopped into_____'s _____, blasting _____ on the
PERON'S NAME   VEHICLE   SONG TITLE

way.

Our first stop was _____ , where we searched for the perfect
STORE NAME

gift for_____. I found a_____ that was _____ enough to
CELEBRITY NAME   NOUN   ADJECTIVE

make them _____ with excitement! Next, we headed to the food
VERB

court to grab_____, but _____ accidentally spilled _____all
FOOD   PERON'S NAME   LIQUID

over their _____ . We couldn't stop laughing!
CLOTHING ITEM

After that, we went to _____ to look for some _____ .
STORE NAME   PLURAL NOUN

We saw the most _____ holiday sweaters, and of course, we all had to
ADJECTIVE

try them on and take a _____ in the mirror.
VERB

By the end of the day, our bags were full of_____, and we
PLURAL NOUN

had spent _____ dollars on the weirdest things. But the best part was
NUMBER

_____ with my friends and making memories we'll laugh about
VERB ENDING IN ING

until _____ !
HOLIDAY

SANTA SOS

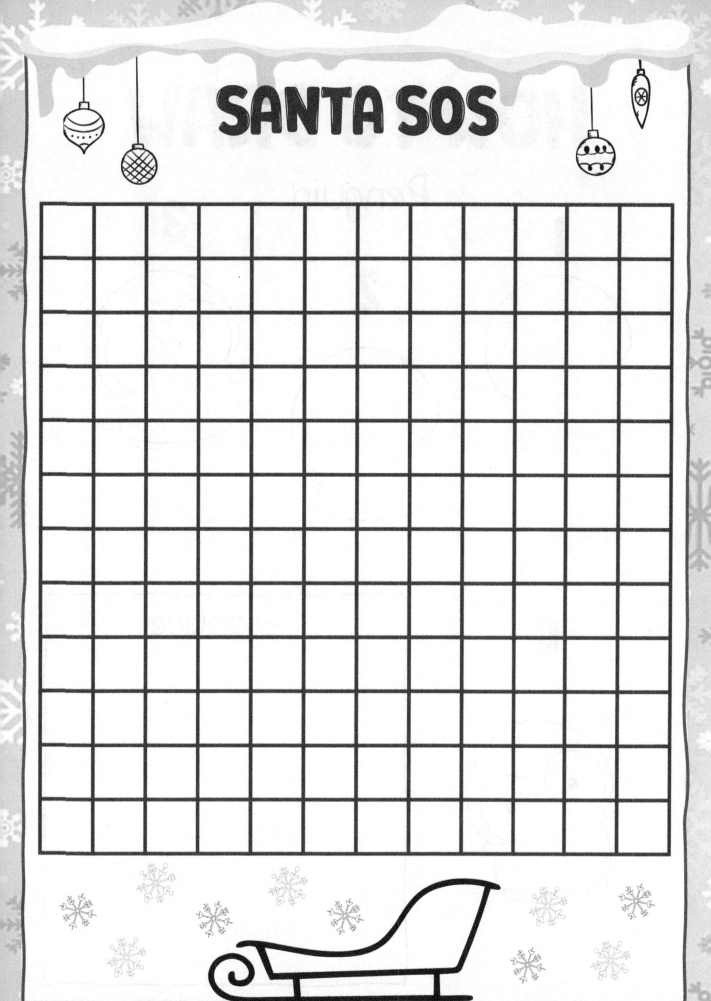

HOW TO DRAW

Penguin

1

2

3

4

Practice

EASY SUDOKU

Puzzle 1

	5				9	8		6
6		4		1	5	3	2	7
	8	2	6	7	3	4	5	
5	4	6		8				3
		8			4		6	1
9	1		5	6	7			
4	3	5	7	9		1		
			2	4	8		3	
8		9	3		1		7	4

Puzzle 2

3	8	2	7	4				6
9	4	1	3		2			
	7		8		9	3	4	
			6	9	4	7		
7	6	8	2	5	3	4	9	1
4	9	5	1	8	7	6	2	3
	3	4	5		6		7	
6							5	1
8			4					6

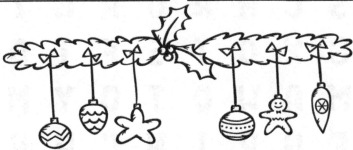

Puzzle 3

3		8			6	2		7
	2		8				1	3
5	6	7	3	2	1	8		
1	7						8	2
4	9	3	5	8	2	1		6
		2			9	5	3	
	3	1	9	6				5
	4		2		5	7		1
		9	7	1	4		6	8

Puzzle 4

6		4	5			1		2
9	2			3	7		8	5
			8			9	1	6
5		8	3	6			4	2
1	6	3			4	7		8
2		9			8		5	3
8	9	2	7	1		6		
7	1	5			6		3	9
		6		2			7	1

WORD SEARCH 2

Christmas Movies

```
H G R E M L I N S K Z L
O R K D L P J O K R T O
M Q R K E R A E L F Q V
E S A N T A C L A U S E
A F M G I N K L U Y C A
L R P N T C F E S L R C
O O U R S E R R W M O T
N S S C N R O H G Z O U
E T G X O T S F I Q G A
P Y M A W Q T O Y M E L
T H E G R I N C H H D L
U T T H E H O L I D A Y
```

Elf	Klaus	Prancer
Frosty	Krampus	Santa Clause
Gremlins	Let It Snow	Scrooged
Home Alone	Love Actually	The Grinch
Jack Frost	Noelle	The Holiday

FREE DRAW

Decorate the Tree.

EVER OR NEVER

	Yes	No

1. Gone on a winter hike?
2. Had a snow day off from school?
3. Decorated gingerbread house?
4. Gone snowtubing?
5. Helped hang lights outside your house?
6. Been to a holiday parade?
7. Taken a pic with Santa?
8. Made Christmas ornaments?
9. Spent Christmas away from home?
10. Worn matching pajamas for Christmas?
11. Stayed up all night on Christmas eve?
12. Exchanged gifts with friends?
13. Donated items during the season?
14. Gone on a horse-drawn sleigh ride?
15. Opened a Christmas gift early?
16. Made a snow angel in the snow?
17. Tried ice fishing in the winter?
18. Been in a Christmas play?
19. Tried to find hidden gifts?
20. Stayed up till midnight new years eve?

Points total:

FIND THAT WORD

H	O	S	A	N	T
S	C	H	P	C	A
P	P	R	I	S	T
G	E	S	E	A	M
S	T	N	S	I	S
U	F	M	E	T	A

_____

_____

_____

_____

_____

3 or 4 letters......1 point ✳ 5 letters......2 points ✳ 6 letters......3 points
✳ 7 letters......4 points ✳ 8 or more is 10 points ✳ TOTAL: _____ ✳

SANTA SOS

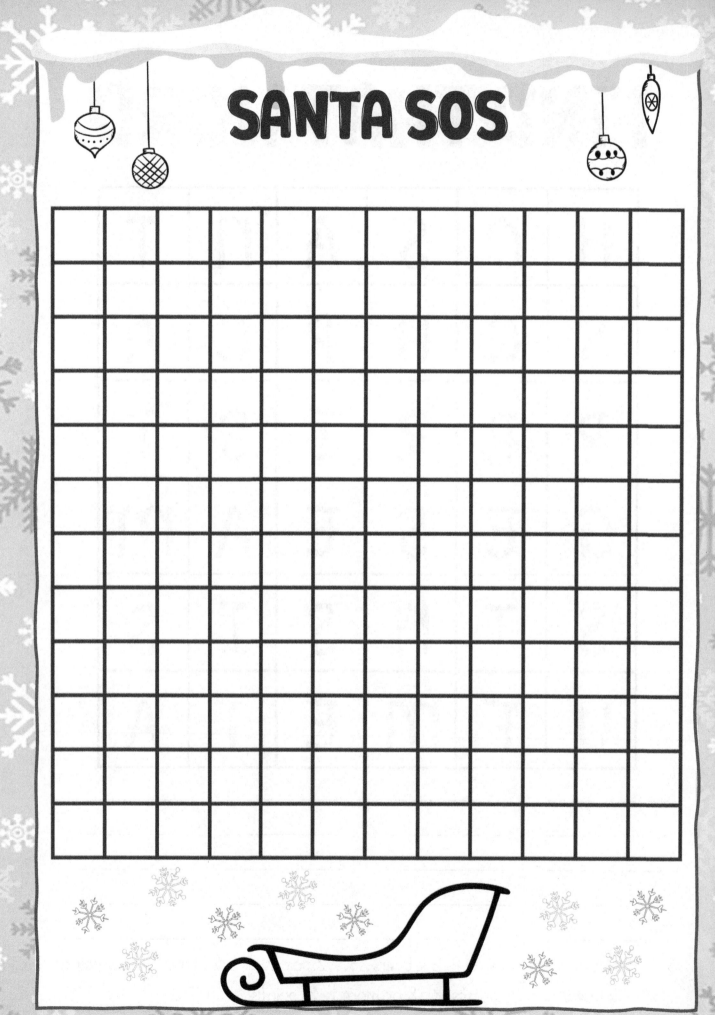

MAZE #2

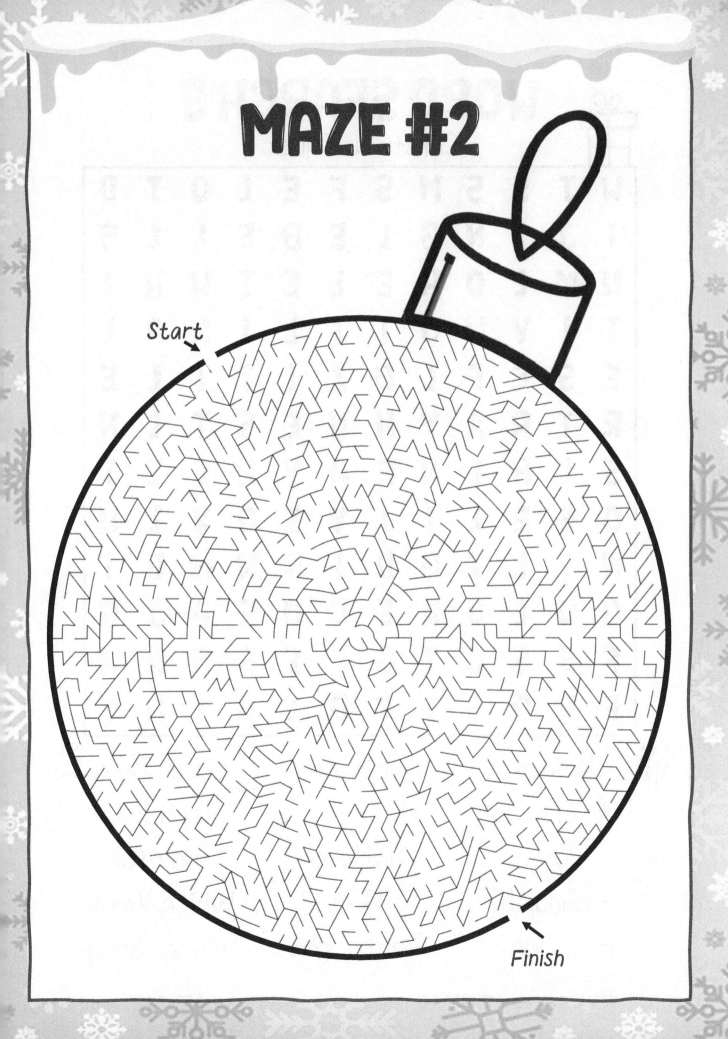

Start

Finish

WORD SEARCH 3
Christmas Music

```
W T S S M S F E L O T D
I J I N G L E B E L L S
N M L O H E L E T W H I
T I V W O I L I H A L E
E S E F L G Z I T I L N
R T R A Y H N E S T L N
S L B L N R A V N E E T
O E E L I I V E O X L N
N T L T G D I N W M U I
G O L U H E D O R A J G
F E S C T B A E S S A H
F R O S T Y D L D I H T
```

 Believe

Feliz Navidad

Frosty

Hallelujah

Holy Night

Jingle Bells

Let It Snow

Mistletoe

Noel

Silent Night

Silver Bells

Sleigh Ride

Snowfall

White Xmas

Winter Song

XMAS WORDPLAY

The Great Christmas Dinner

Christmas dinner at _____'s house is always _____ . This
_____RELATIVE'S NAME_____   ___ADJECTIVE___

year, the table was covered in _____ and decorated with _____
                                ___PLURAL NOUN___   ___COLOR___

lights. We all sat down, and _____ served a huge plate of _____ ,
                              ___RELATIVE'S NAME___   ___FOOD___

which smelled like _____ .
                   ___SCENT___

  I took a bite, and immediately _____ . It tasted like _____
                                 ___VERB ENDING IN ED___   ___NOUN___

mixed with _____ ! _____ whispered, "This is more _____ than
           ___FOOD___ ___RELATIVE'S NAME___   ___ADJECTIVE___

last year's _____ disaster."
            ___NOUN___

  After dinner, we all gathered to open presents. I got a _____
                                                          ___ADJECTIVE___

_____ from _____ , which I pretended to love. _____
___GIFT ITEM___   ___RELATIVE'S NAME___   ___RELATIVE'S NAME___

however, couldn't hide their surprise when they unwrapped a _____
                                                            ___ADJECTIVE___

_____ that made everyone _____ . Finally, we finished the night with
___NOUN___   ___VERB___

_____ for dessert, and _____ accidentally set the _____
___PLURAL NOUN___   ___RELATIVE'S NAME___   ___OBJECT___

on fire with a _____ candle! Everyone was laughing so hard, we nearly
               ___ADJECTIVE___

forgot about the _____ we had planned after dinner.
                 ___HOLIDAY ACTIVITY___

  Christmas dinners with my family are _____ , and I wouldn't
                                       ___ADJECTIVE___

change them for the world!

THE GAME OF SIM

CONNECT THE DOTS

EVER OR NEVER

	Yes	No

1. Gone to a winter event?
2. Made hot chocolate from scratch?
3. Tried making snow ice cream?
4. Worn Christmas-themed accessories?
5. Taken a family Christmas photo?
6. Gone on a winter vacation?
7. Written a letter to Santa?
8. Gone to see a Christmas ballet?
9. Made a DIY Christmas gift?
10. Spent Christmas in a different country?
11. Helped prepare Christmas dinner?
12. Had a video call with relatives?
13. Had a snowstorm cancel a plan?
14. Watched a holiday special on tv?
15. Bought a gift with your own money?
16. Worn Christmas nail art or makeup?
17. Played holiday video games or apps?
18. Decorated a classroom for Christmas?
19. Hosted a holiday game night?
20. Gone window shopping?

Points total:

FREE DRAW

Decorate the gingerbread cookie.

MAZE #3

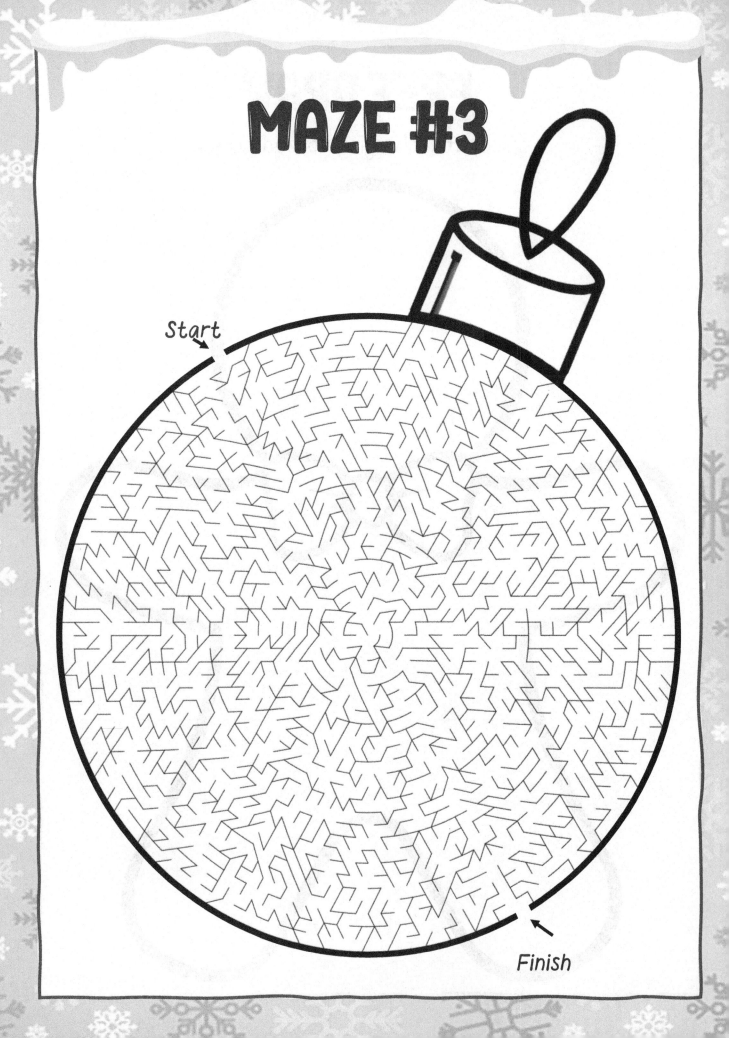

Start

Finish

WORD SEARCH 4
Winter Break Activities

S	B	J	G	D	Y	P	V	M	Z	C	I
K	I	S	L	E	E	P	O	V	E	R	C
I	N	L	U	C	Z	Q	L	Z	I	A	E
P	G	E	G	O	N	L	U	B	Y	F	S
Q	E	D	Z	R	O	F	N	O	F	T	K
P	W	D	Y	A	Y	N	T	W	T	K	A
S	A	I	B	T	K	O	E	R	C	D	T
R	T	N	J	E	Z	T	E	I	Q	R	E
E	C	G	Z	W	N	H	R	T	W	B	I
S	H	B	O	N	F	I	R	E	A	D	Q
P	E	B	A	K	E	N	S	H	O	P	K
P	Q	Z	H	X	U	G	A	M	I	N	G

Bake	Gaming	Ski
Binge Watch	Ice Skate	Sledding
Bonfire	Nothing	Sleepover
Craft	Read	Volunteer
Decorate	Shop	Write

SANTA SOS

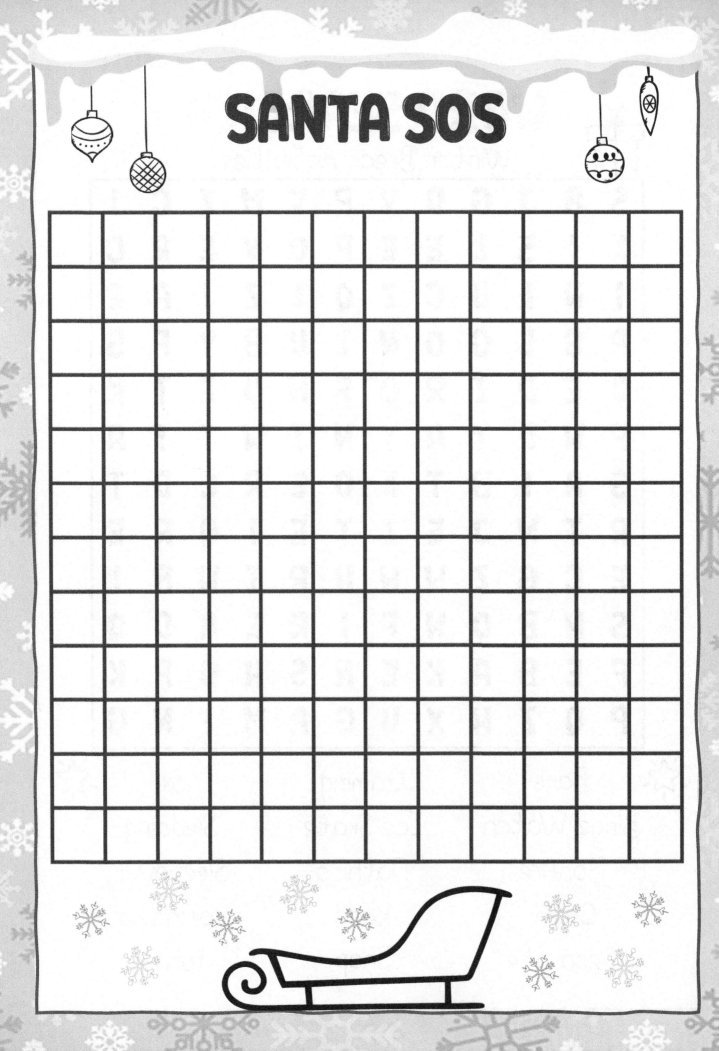

FREE DRAW

Decorate the snowman.

THE GAME OF SiM

XMAS WORDPLAY

Santa's Christmas Morning Visit

On Christmas morning, I woke up to the sound of _____ footsteps on

ANIMAL

the roof. I jumped out of bed and saw a _____ glow coming from the

COLOR

_____ . I crept downstairs and couldn't believe my eyes, there was

ROOM IN HOUSE

Santa Claus, wearing a _____ suit and munching on _____ !

ADJECTIVE   SNACK FOOD

He looked at me and said, "Ho Ho Ho! I almost forgot to leave you

a _____ ." Then, he pulled out a _____ gift wrapped in _____

NOUN   ADJECTIVE   PATTERN

paper. I was so _____ that I almost _____ .

EMOTION   VERB ENDING IN ED

Santa then turned to the _____ , where he saw my pet

PIECE OF FURNITURE

_____ wearing a _____ . Santa chuckled and said, "I have a

ANIMAL   HOLIDAY ACCESSORY

special gift for you, too, little _____ !" He handed my pet a

ANIMAL

_____ _____ , which made them _____ with excitement.

ADJECTIVE   OBJECT   VERB

Before he left, Santa whispered, "Keep being _____ and remember

ADJECTIVE

to always _____ ." And with a _____ , he disappeared up the

VERB   SOUND

chimney, leaving behind a _____ scent of _____ .

SMELL   FOOD

That morning, Christmas was even more _____ because I got to

ADJECTIVE

meet Santa himself!

WORD SEARCH 5

All Things Santa

```
Q  G  N  A  U  G  H  T  Y  P  O  R
W  W  O  R  K  S  H  O  P  R  C  W
M  G  R  E  I  N  D  E  E  R  G  G
C  S  T  O  C  K  I  N  G  S  R  D
O  K  H  A  O  C  H  I  M  N  E  Y
C  V  P  J  O  L  L  Y  A  I  D  H
X  C  O  S  K  I  N  D  G  C  S  Q
N  S  L  E  I  G  H  H  I  E  U  E
I  J  E  L  E  I  O  L  C  I  I  M
F  U  Q  V  S  F  B  V  L  Y  T  I
M  P  A  E  J  T  K  W  L  J  Q  C
B  G  I  S  T  S  D  X  Y  E  P  N
```

Chimney	Kind	Red Suit
Cookies	Magic	Reindeer
Elves	Naughty	Sleigh
Gifts	Nice	Stockings
Jolly	North Pole	Workshop

SANTA SOS

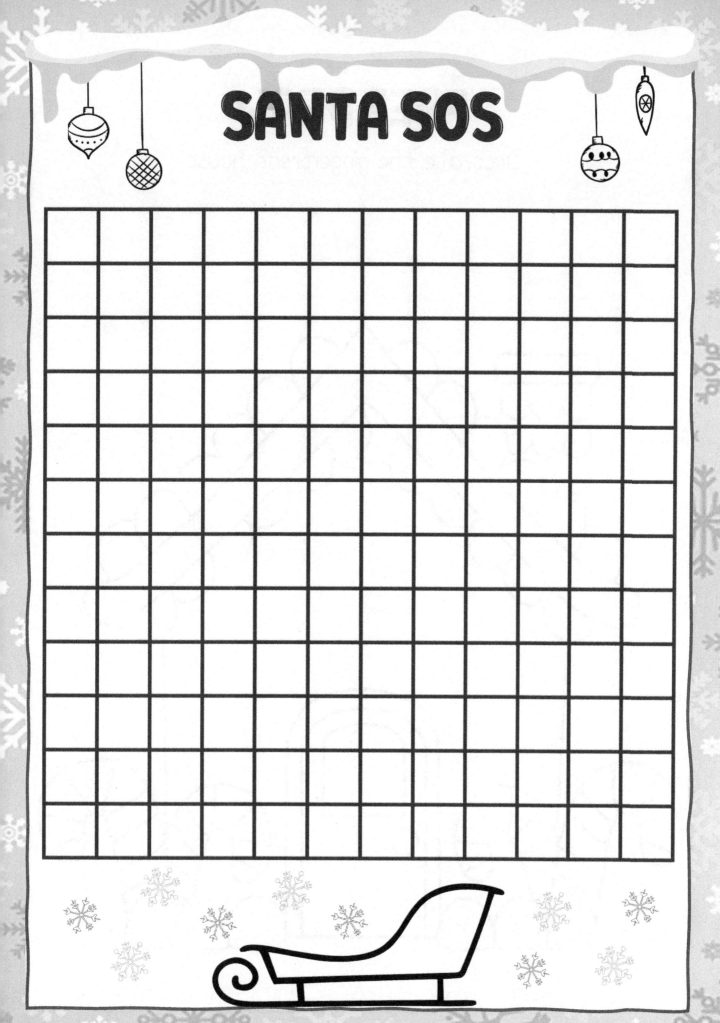

FREE DRAW

Decorate the gingerbread house.

FiND THAT WORD

S	H	O	P	N	G
F	I	G	P	I	A
T	O	O	D	A	C
S	O	Y	E	T	E
A	T	N	S	V	I
N	T	A	E	I	T

_____   _____

_____   _____

_____   _____

_____   _____

3 or 4 letters......1 point ✷ 5 letters......2 points ✷ 6 letters.......3 points
✷ 7 letters.......4 points ✷ 8 or more is 10 points ✷ TOTAL: _____ ✷

HOW TO DRAW

Donut

1

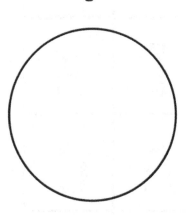

2

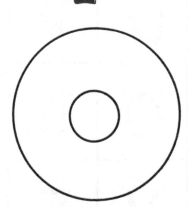

3

4

Practice

MEDIUM SUDOKU

Puzzle 1 (top-left)

3	2		4		5			8
8	7		2		1	4	6	
6				7				2
7			3	1				6
	8	2	6		9	3	5	
	3			8				1
4	9		1			7	2	5
	6			5	4	1		
5	1			2	8	6	3	4

Puzzle 2 (top-right)

2				1	6			
	5	1			2	8	7	
6	4					5	2	1
5		7	6	1		4		9
	9					6	5	
8		2	9			1	3	
		6	5	4		7	1	8
	1	5	8	3	6	2	9	4
4		9				1	3	

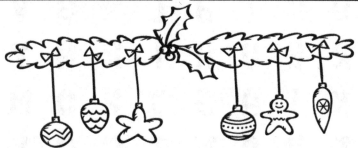

Puzzle 3 (bottom-left)

2		8	5					6
3		4			9	5		
9	6			2		4		8
6	3		4		8			5
5	9	7			2	8		4
4	8	2		5	6	1	7	3
7		9		3	5			1
8		3	1		7	2	4	
1			8	9			5	

Puzzle 4 (bottom-right)

3	6		8	9	4	5		2
4		5	7	1		8		
	8	7			5	1	3	4
			7	1		3	2	
7	1	3	9	2	8	4	5	6
		2	3	4	6	7		1
5						6	4	3
	7	8						
2				3				7

WORD SEARCH 6
Christmas Goodies

```
J B G F N G C B R Z G V
B B O R O A S T E I I C
O S P U D D I N G M N A
X U K I N K A T A V G N
U L S T U F F I N G E D
M C S C R A N B E R R Y
P O T A T O E S G A B U
I O U K T B L N G V R L
E K R E U H I R N Y E E
N I K I A J J F O M A L
S E E H A M Z G G Y D O
D S Y J Q O G V R F T G
```

 Candy   Gingerbread   Pudding

Cookies   Gravy   Roast

Cranberry   Ham   Stuffing

Eggnog   Pie   Turkey

Fruitcake   Potatoes   Yule Log

FREE DRAW

Decorate your own ornament.

THE GAME OF SiM

HOW TO DRAW

Candle

1

2

3

4

Practice

CONNECT THE DOTS

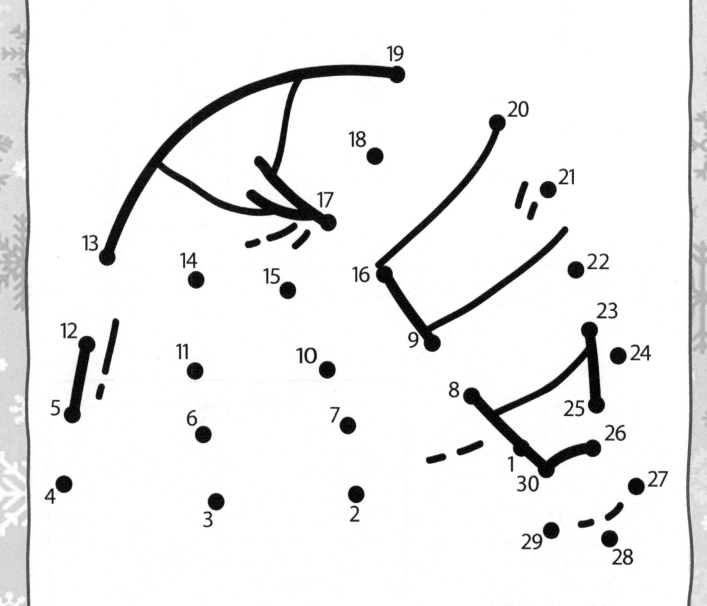

MAZE #4

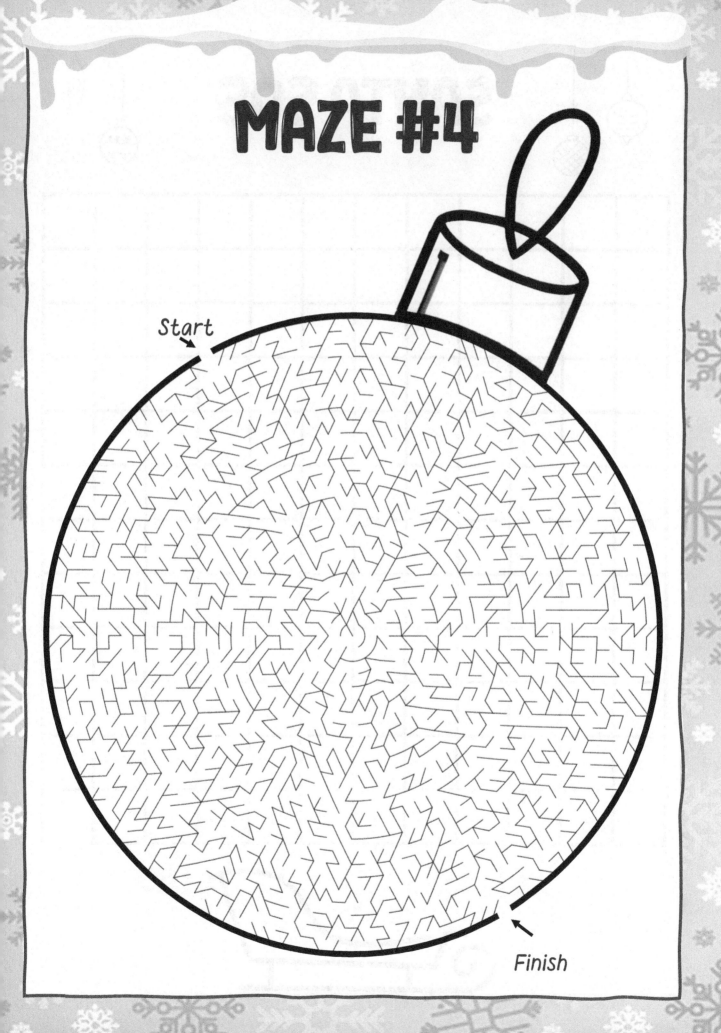

Start

Finish

SANTA SOS

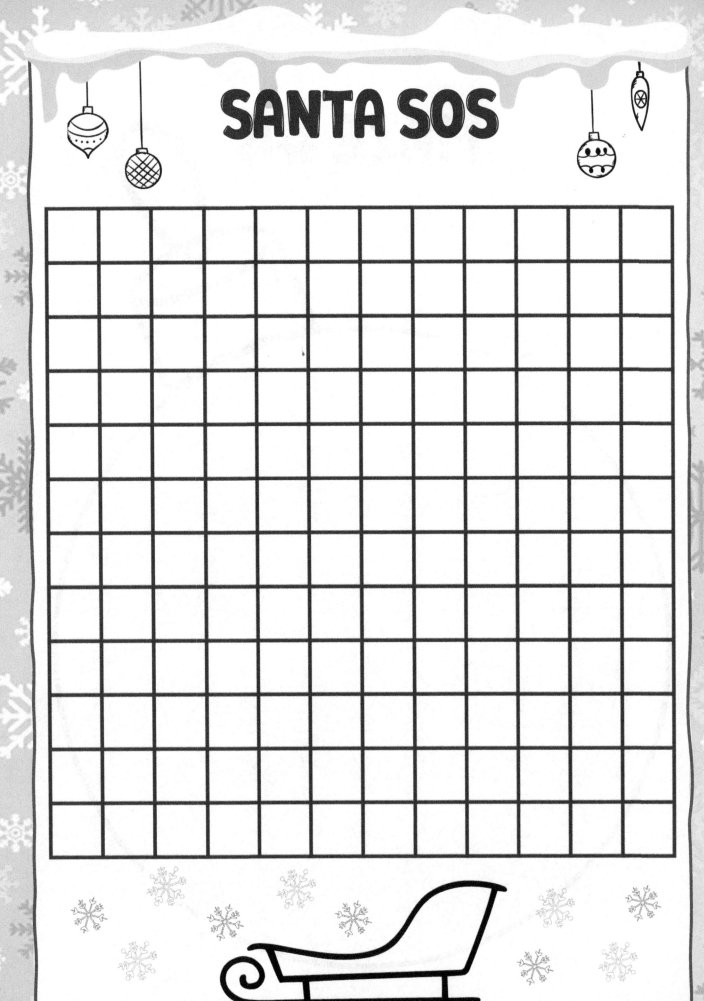

EVER OR NEVER

Yes | No

1. Used an advent calendar?
2. Gone shopping on black friday?
3. Been in a Christmas talent show?
4. Watched light displays set to music?
5. Done a holiday-themed DIY craft?
6. Donated food to a holiday food drive?
7. Been involved in a charity event?
8. Built a fort indoors during winter?
9. Helped bake a Christmas cake or pie?
10. Surprised someone with a joke gift?
11. Decorated your room for Christmas?
12. Gone to a midnight mass?
13. Left cookies and milk out for Santa?
14. Hosted a winter sleepover?
15. Used a winter filter on social media?
16. Attended a winter dance?
17. Created a holiday playlist?
18. Gone on a holiday scavenger hunt?
19. Spent a day watching Christmas movies?
20. Gone to a Christmas tree lighting ceremony?

Points total:

XMAS WORDPLAY

My First Ice Skating Adventure

Today, I went ice skating for the first time at _____ , and it

PLACE

was _____ ! I put on a pair of _____ skates that felt like

ADJECTIVE   COLOR

_____ on my feet. As soon as I stepped onto the ice, I

PLURAL NOUN

started to _____ uncontrollably.

VERB

_____ was with me and shouted, "Just_____ like a

FRIEND'S NAME   VERB

_____ !" But as I tried to glide, I ended up _____ right

ANIMAL   VERB ENDING IN ING

into a _____ ! Everyone around me started _____ , and I

OBJECT   VERB ENDING IN ING

felt as red as a _____ .

FRUIT

After a few _____ , I finally got the hang of it — sort

PLURAL NOUN

of. _____ and I decided to try a _____ spin, but we ended

FRIEND'S NAME   ADJECTIVE

up crashing into _____ other skaters who were carrying

NUMBER

_____ !

PLURAL NOUN

By the end, I was _____ but proud. Ice skating was more

EMOTION

_____ than I expected, and I can't wait to _____ again

ADJECTIVE   VERB

next time — hopefully without falling like a _____ !

FUNNY ANIMAL

WORD SEARCH 7
Gifts We All Want

```
F U R N I T U R E G P C
F G I F T C A R D S R O
G A M I N G S Y S T E M
I M O B A V C K C E E P
R I N U D R L H H L M U
I N E B N S O F O E P T
M G Y N D Y T E C V S E
I B D B E S H P O I P R
P U O C T T E E L S U V
A C G A M E S E A I S K
N K J T L M D Y T O A W
Y S H V T R Q H E N H U
```

Car	Dog	Gift Cards
Cat	Furniture	Money
Chocolate	Games	SUV
Clothes	Gaming Bucks	Television
Computer	Gaming System	VR System

FREE DRAW

Decorate the Tree.

HOW TO DRAW

Fire

1

2

3

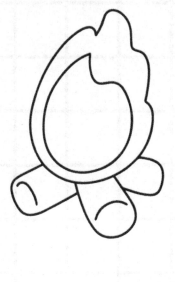

4

Practice

SANTA SOS

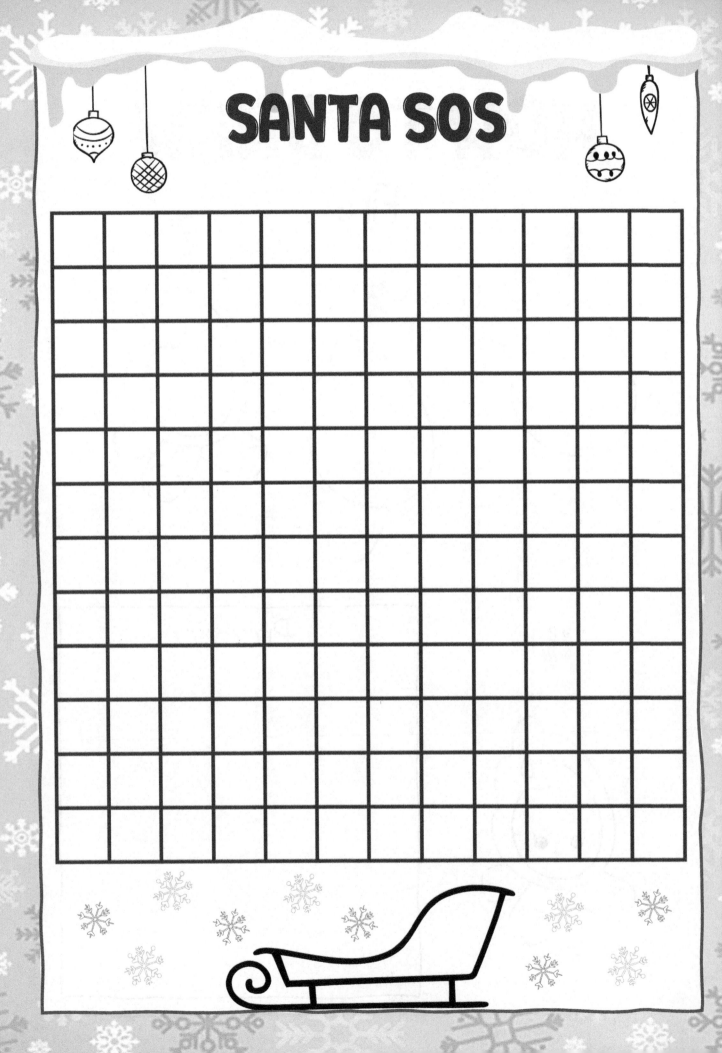

HARD SUDOKU

Puzzle 1

		7	5				2	1
9			8	4		5	6	
6	8			7		3		
8						7		2
		9	4	8			3	
7	6		3					
	9	2	7				1	8
			5	1			9	
1	3		2	9	6		5	4

Puzzle 2

3				6	8		2	7
5				3		6	8	1
	4	6					1	
	7	5		9		4		
6		9	3		1	7		
1		4	6	7			9	
4	9			1		2		
5	1		2	3		4		
		3				1		5

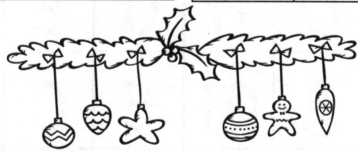

Puzzle 3

	1	9	3		6			
	5	3	1			6	7	
6	8		7			1	5	
	6	1	9		7	5	2	
		7		3	4			1
				5	3	9		
	3	6						
		8				1	2	
1	7		8		2	4		6

Puzzle 4

	5		6			8		
6	3		7	1			4	9
			5				6	3
2	9		3			4	8	7
4				9	7	1	5	6
	6		1	8	4			2
	4							5
					1			
1	7	4	2	5	6			

FIND THAT WORD

P	S	K	I	P	O
I	M	E	A	N	L
A	A	C	T	D	I
R	O	H	U	E	N
E	B	M	E	C	n
n	T	A	E	R	E

_____ _____ _____ _____

_____ _____ _____ _____

_____ _____ _____ _____

_____ _____ _____ _____

3 or 4 letters......1 point ✳ 5 letters......2 points ✳ 6 letters......3 points
✳ 7 letters......4 points ✳ 8 or more is 10 points ✳ TOTAL: _____ ✳

WORD SEARCH 8
Traditions

```
T R E E L I G H T I N G
G R G U H F M C J G Z I
E D Q E F O I H O U C F
S E C R E T S A N T A T
T C A T A D T R A R C G
O O R W S I L I T A H I
C R O A T N E T I B U V
K A L D I N T Y V A R I
I T I V N E O U I K C N
N I N E G R E O T I H G
G N G N A K A T Y N E A
S G A T H E R I N G S Q
```

Advent   Decorating   Mistletoe

Baking   Dinner   Nativity

Caroling   Feasting   Secret Santa

Charity   Gatherings   Stockings

Church   Gift Giving   Tree Lighting

FREE DRAW

Fill the empty present with your most wished for item.

CONNECT THE DOTS

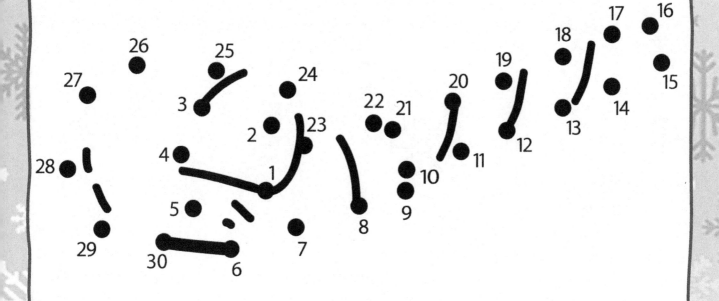

THE GAME OF SiM

SOLUTIONS

EASY SOLUTIONS

3	5	7	4	2	9	8	1	6
6	9	4	8	1	5	3	2	7
1	8	2	6	7	3	4	5	9
5	4	6	1	8	2	7	9	3
2	7	8	9	3	4	5	6	1
9	1	3	5	6	7	2	4	8
4	3	5	7	9	6	1	8	2
7	6	1	2	4	8	9	3	5
8	2	9	3	5	1	6	7	4

3	8	2	7	4	5	1	6	9
9	4	1	3	6	2	8	5	7
5	7	6	8	1	9	3	4	2
2	1	3	6	9	4	7	8	5
7	6	8	2	5	3	4	9	1
4	9	5	1	8	7	6	2	3
1	3	4	5	2	6	9	7	8
6	2	7	9	3	8	5	1	4
8	5	9	4	7	1	2	3	6

3	1	8	4	9	6	2	5	7
9	2	4	8	5	7	6	1	3
5	6	7	3	2	1	8	4	9
1	7	5	6	4	3	9	8	2
4	9	3	5	8	2	1	7	6
6	8	2	1	7	9	5	3	4
7	3	1	9	6	8	4	2	5
8	4	6	2	3	5	7	9	1
2	5	9	7	1	4	3	6	8

6	8	4	5	9	1	3	2	7
9	2	1	6	3	7	4	8	5
3	5	7	4	8	2	9	1	6
5	7	8	3	6	9	1	4	2
1	6	3	2	5	4	7	9	8
2	4	9	1	7	8	6	5	3
8	9	2	7	1	3	5	6	4
7	1	5	8	4	6	2	3	9
4	3	6	9	2	5	8	7	1

MEDIUM SOLUTIONS

3	2	1	4	6	5	9	7	8
8	7	5	2	9	1	4	6	3
6	4	9	8	7	3	5	1	2
7	5	4	3	1	2	8	9	6
1	8	2	6	4	9	3	5	7
9	3	6	5	8	7	2	4	1
4	9	8	1	3	6	7	2	5
2	6	3	7	5	4	1	8	9
5	1	7	9	2	8	6	3	4

2	7	8	1	6	5	9	4	3
9	5	1	4	2	3	8	7	6
6	4	3	7	9	8	5	2	1
5	3	7	6	1	2	4	8	9
1	9	4	3	8	7	6	5	2
8	6	2	9	5	4	1	3	7
3	2	6	5	4	9	7	1	8
7	1	5	8	3	6	2	9	4
4	8	9	2	7	1	3	6	5

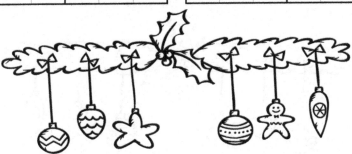

2	1	8	5	4	3	7	9	6
3	7	4	6	8	9	5	1	2
9	6	5	7	2	1	4	3	8
6	3	1	4	7	8	9	2	5
5	9	7	3	1	2	8	6	4
4	8	2	9	5	6	1	7	3
7	4	9	2	3	5	6	8	1
8	5	3	1	6	7	2	4	9
1	2	6	8	9	4	3	5	7

1	3	6	8	9	4	5	7	2
4	2	5	7	1	3	8	6	9
9	8	7	6	5	2	1	3	4
6	4	9	5	7	1	3	2	8
7	1	3	9	2	8	4	5	6
8	5	2	3	4	6	7	9	1
5	9	1	2	8	7	6	4	3
3	7	8	4	6	9	2	1	5
2	6	4	1	3	5	9	8	7

HARD SOLUTIONS

3	4	7	6	5	9	8	2	1
9	2	1	8	4	3	5	6	7
6	8	5	1	7	2	3	4	9
8	1	3	9	6	5	4	7	2
2	5	9	4	8	7	1	3	6
7	6	4	3	2	1	9	8	5
5	9	2	7	3	4	6	1	8
4	7	6	5	1	8	2	9	3
1	3	8	2	9	6	7	5	4

9	3	1	4	6	8	5	2	7
7	5	2	1	3	9	6	8	4
8	4	6	2	5	7	3	1	9
3	7	5	8	9	2	4	6	1
6	8	9	3	4	1	7	5	2
1	2	4	6	7	5	8	9	3
4	9	7	5	1	6	2	3	8
5	1	8	7	2	3	9	4	6
2	6	3	9	8	4	1	7	5

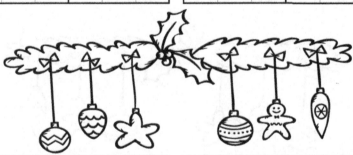

7	1	9	3	5	6	2	4	8
4	5	3	1	2	8	6	7	9
6	8	2	7	4	9	1	5	3
3	6	1	9	8	7	5	2	4
5	9	7	2	3	4	8	6	1
8	2	4	6	1	5	3	9	7
2	3	6	4	7	1	9	8	5
9	4	8	5	6	3	7	1	2
1	7	5	8	9	2	4	3	6

9	5	4	6	3	8	7	2	1
6	3	8	7	1	2	5	4	9
1	7	2	5	4	9	8	6	3
2	9	1	3	5	6	4	8	7
4	8	3	2	9	7	1	5	6
7	6	5	1	8	4	9	3	2
8	4	6	9	7	3	2	1	5
5	2	9	8	6	1	3	7	4
3	1	7	4	2	5	6	9	8

SOLUTIONS

PUZZLE 1

PUZZLE 2

PUZZLE 3

PUZZLE 4

WORD SEARCH SOLUTIONS

1

C	A	M	M	W	W	F	A	M	I	L	Y
O	T	U	N	P	R	E	S	E	N	T	S
O	K	S	X	A	A	S	U	E	H	R	E
K	A	I	Z	J	P	T	R	E	E	A	H
I	B	C	I	A	P	I	P	Y	X	D	L
E	F	A	M	M	I	V	R	B	J	I	A
S	V	N	J	A	N	E	I	J	A	T	U
F	S	D	D	S	G	F	S	X	C	I	G
I	L	L	D	V	X	T	E	G	B	O	H
P	Q	E	X	C	I	T	E	M	E	N	T
N	H	S	T	O	C	K	I	N	G	S	E
X	U	W	A	R	M	T	H	U	B	I	R

2

H	G	R	E	M	L	I	N	S	K	Z	L
O	R	K	D	L	P	J	O	K	R	T	O
M	Q	R	K	E	R	A	E	L	F	Q	V
E	S	A	N	T	A	C	L	A	U	S	E
A	F	M	G	I	N	K	L	U	Y	C	A
L	R	P	N	T	C	F	E	S	L	R	C
O	O	U	R	S	E	R	R	W	M	O	T
N	S	S	C	N	R	O	H	G	Z	O	U
E	T	G	X	O	T	S	F	I	Q	G	A
P	Y	M	A	W	Q	T	O	Y	M	E	L
T	H	E	G	R	I	N	C	H	H	D	L
U	T	T	H	E	H	O	L	I	D	A	Y

3

W	T	S	S	M	S	F	E	L	O	T	D
I	J	I	N	G	L	E	B	E	L	L	S
N	M	L	O	H	E	L	E	T	W	H	I
T	I	V	W	O	I	I	L	I	H	A	L
E	S	E	F	L	G	Z	I	T	I	L	E
R	T	R	A	Y	H	N	E	S	T	L	N
S	L	B	L	N	R	A	V	N	E	E	T
O	E	E	L	I	I	V	E	O	X	L	N
N	T	L	T	G	D	I	N	W	M	U	I
G	O	L	U	H	E	D	O	R	A	J	G
F	E	S	C	T	B	A	E	S	S	A	H
F	R	O	S	T	Y	D	L	D	I	H	T

4

S	B	J	G	D	Y	P	V	M	Z	C	I
K	I	S	L	E	E	P	O	V	E	R	C
I	N	L	U	C	Z	Q	L	Z	I	A	E
P	G	E	G	O	N	L	U	B	Y	F	S
Q	E	D	Z	R	O	F	N	O	F	T	K
P	W	D	Y	A	Y	N	T	W	T	T	A
S	A	I	B	T	K	O	E	R	C	D	T
R	T	N	J	E	Z	T	E	I	Q	R	E
E	C	G	Z	W	N	H	R	T	W	B	I
S	H	B	O	N	F	I	R	E	A	D	Q
P	E	B	A	K	E	N	S	H	O	P	K
P	Q	Z	H	X	U	G	A	M	I	N	G

5

Q	G	N	A	U	G	H	T	Y	P	O	R
W	W	O	R	K	S	H	O	P	R	C	W
M	G	R	E	I	N	D	E	E	R	G	G
C	S	T	O	C	K	I	N	G	S	R	D
O	K	H	A	O	C	H	I	M	N	E	Y
C	V	P	J	O	L	L	Y	A	I	D	H
X	C	O	S	K	I	N	D	G	C	S	Q
N	S	L	E	I	G	H	H	I	E	U	E
I	J	E	L	E	I	O	L	C	I	I	M
F	U	Q	V	S	F	B	V	L	Y	T	I
M	P	A	E	J	T	K	W	L	J	Q	C
B	G	I	S	T	S	D	X	Y	E	P	N

6

J	B	G	F	N	G	C	B	R	Z	G	V
B	B	O	R	O	A	S	T	E	I	I	C
O	S	P	U	D	D	I	N	G	M	N	A
X	U	K	I	N	K	A	T	A	V	G	N
U	L	S	T	U	F	F	I	N	G	E	D
M	C	S	C	R	A	N	B	E	R	R	Y
P	O	T	A	T	O	E	S	G	A	B	U
I	O	U	K	T	B	L	N	G	V	R	L
E	K	R	E	U	H	I	R	N	Y	E	E
N	I	K	I	A	J	J	F	O	M	A	L
S	E	E	H	A	M	Z	G	G	Y	D	O
D	S	Y	J	Q	O	G	V	R	F	T	G

7

F	U	R	N	I	T	U	R	E	G	P	C
F	G	I	F	T	C	A	R	D	S	R	O
G	A	M	I	N	G	S	Y	S	T	E	M
I	M	O	B	A	V	C	K	C	E	E	P
R	I	N	U	D	R	L	H	H	L	M	U
I	N	E	B	N	S	O	F	O	E	P	T
M	G	Y	N	D	Y	T	E	C	V	S	E
I	B	D	B	E	S	H	P	O	I	P	R
P	U	O	C	T	T	E	E	L	S	U	V
A	C	G	A	M	E	S	E	A	I	S	K
N	K	J	T	L	M	D	Y	T	O	A	W
Y	S	H	V	T	R	Q	H	E	N	H	U

8

T	R	E	E	L	I	G	H	T	I	N	G
G	R	G	U	H	F	M	C	J	G	Z	I
E	D	Q	E	F	O	I	H	O	U	C	F
S	E	C	R	E	T	S	A	N	T	A	T
T	C	A	T	A	D	T	R	A	R	C	G
O	O	R	W	S	I	L	I	T	A	H	I
C	R	O	A	T	N	E	T	I	B	U	V
K	A	L	D	I	N	T	Y	V	A	R	I
I	T	I	V	N	E	O	U	I	K	C	N
N	I	N	E	G	R	E	O	T	I	H	G
G	N	G	N	A	K	A	T	Y	N	E	A
S	G	A	T	H	E	R	I	N	G	S	Q

Made in the USA
Las Vegas, NV
05 December 2024

13416940R00059